In the Shadows of God

Mission: To Proclaim Transformation and Truth

Published by: Transformed Publishing
Website: www.transformedpublishing.com
Email: transformedpublishing@gmail.com

Copyright © 2021 by Raven Simone Caples

All rights reserved solely by the author. No part of this book may be reproduced, stored in a retrieval system, or transmitted in any form or by any means without expressed written permission of the author.

Permission granted to Raven Simone Caples to use excerpt from the Community of Hope website. Retrieved on 4/3/21 from: https://www.hopeofbrevard.com/index.php/stories/

Scripture is taken from the New King James Version ®, unless otherwise noted. Copyright © 1982 by Thomas Nelson. Used by permission. All rights reserved.

As noted (KJV), scripture is taken from the King James Bible ®, Public Domain.

ISBN: 978-1-953241-10-8
Printed in the U.S.A.

In the Shadows of God

Raven Simone Caples

Dedication

This book is dedicated to women of all ages, younger and older, who are struggling or have struggled with addictions, lust, suicide, peer pressure, and other dark issues.

Because God is Sovereign...

Noah (my baby)

He's wise, beautiful, smart, caring, & strong. He will do wonderful things in the Kingdom of God. This is why God said, "Name him Noah."

Kye (my second oldest)

He's bold, brave, & very wise. He's mommy's future entrepreneur. He will do great things for the Kingdom of God. He's very rare.

Destiny (my oldest)

She's my reflection of better and great Destiny. She's beautiful, smart, caring, & bold. She is my better me. My flower. She will do great things for the Kingdom of God

Us

Acknowledgements

I want it to be known that I support all strong women that are doing their best while trusting God and keeping Him first.

The purpose of this book is to share my story. As I share the circumstances I faced growing up, I want each person who encounters this book to see the difference between trusting God and just doing *it* on their own. I realize that with God everything is possible.

I am fortunate to have this understanding at a young age: the goal God has for me and His plan must be the forefront of my life. It is only fair that I share my experience to help others.

But Jesus looked at them and said to them, "with men this is impossible, but with God all things are possible."

Matthew 19:26

Table of Contents

1. Remembering My Father 1
2. Introduction 3
3. Living with My Mother & Stepdad 5
4. Living on My Own 9
5. Rape 13
6. Taking Care of My Mother 19
7. Becoming a Mother 23
8. Health Issues 27
9. Saying Goodbye 31
10. Rebellion 35
11. My Struggles 39
12. Being a Single Mom Through It All .. 43
13. Having Standards 47
14. My Last Thoughts 51

    The God of the Impossible 53

    Stay in Touch 57

1

Remembering My Father

I was born July 14, 1993 and am the second oldest of four siblings. Growing up my childhood was very chaotic, and I faced many hardships at a young age. However, my father was my safe haven. My father named me after a famous actress. He just knew his baby girl was going to be great.

My father and mother separated, and she remarried when I was 5 years old. Despite my parents failed relationship I was still close to my biological father and he used to get me every weekend. My father was my hero, he was also very strict. He really stressed the importance of education and was very hard on me. In his mind he wanted the best for me. So, he pushed me. It wasn't always comfortable, but I knew he loved me. I knew he loved me because he would always speak about me to family members and took so many pictures of me. I believe it was hard for my father because he couldn't be the father he desired to be. My mother had full custody and he only had partial. He was doing the best he could with what he had been given.

Now with kids of my own, I sometimes wonder how he would have felt about being a grandpa. Unfortunately, I'll never know because in 2004 he passed away in his sleep. I learned later that he was born with congestive heart failure. He was only 49 years old when he passed away and I was just 11 years old.

2

Introduction

This book is about my life thus far and all the challenges I had to face but overcame with the Lord. Faith is something we vocalize often but don't practice. It's similar to the word *love*. We say it often but is it *really* felt by others? Do we put love in to action? Believing that I would overcome the adversities in my life was only half the battle. I also needed to move in my faith in the Lord to overcome. In Revelation 2:7 the bible states, "He who has an ear, let him hear what the Spirit says to the churches. To him who overcomes I will give to eat from the tree of life, which is in the midst of the Paradise of God." To overcome is not for anybody - it is for you.

Remember you have somewhere to go and a place to be. That's with your heavenly Father. My hope in sharing my story is that you get encouragement and wisdom along the way.

3

Living with My Mother & Stepdad

Growing up my childhood wasn't ideal. However, the mental, physical, emotional, and spiritual growth that I obtained from it has shaped me into the woman I am today. During the fifteen years my mother was married to my stepdad I endured many hardships. My stepdad battled with drug addiction the entire time they were married, and it really affected the stability in our home. Even though he played the role of the father figure in the house his drug addiction always took over.

I remember my mother working long shifts to keep food on the table and working even harder to keep all the bills paid. She would constantly try to figure out how she would get home from work while my stepdad stayed home and did not contribute to her well-being.

Basically, my mom was a single parent. She just lived with a roommate that happened to be her husband. At least that's how I looked at it. A husband wouldn't be verbally and physically abusive like my stepdad, *would they?* In spite of it all, my mother stayed with him and I could hear the frustration in her voice and how heartbroken she was over his actions.

My oldest brother lived with us at the time and I really looked up to him. He, however, was my mother's troubled child and was in the streets. He was selling drugs and in a gang at the time. Even though I knew it wasn't right, I always felt protected and safe when I was with him. I didn't feel that way with my mother, so I clung to my brother.

I resented and hated my mother growing up because she chose a man over her own children. It wasn't fair or right, and I verbalized that to her every chance I could. She didn't like that, and we would get into physical fights. She would punch and fight me like I was her enemy, not her daughter. The rejection I felt from my mother fueled me to be rebellious and I didn't want to listen to anything she had to say.

However, I did have one outlet which was school. I enjoyed going and did any extra work I could to take my mind off of my life at home. At this particular time in my life, I was often reminded of this scripture, "The sacrifices of God are a broken spirit: a broken and a contrite heart, O God, thou wilt not despise (Psalm 51:17, KJV). Even in your brokenness, God still and will use you.

4

Living on My Own

I lived with my mother and stepdad until I was 18 years old. Honestly, that's all I could take. My mom apparently felt the same because she decided to kick me out.

It was my senior year of high school and I was preparing for graduation. I was doing really well in school. So well, that I was awarded a 4-year scholarship from an essay I wrote about living with a parent on drugs. *Who would have thought me venting on a piece of paper would land me a scholarship?* Proverbs 18:16 was proven in my life, "A man's gift maketh room for him, and bringeth him before great men" (KJV).

Unfortunately, that excitement was short lived. When I came home from school one day, I found out my mother was packing to move. I was told I wasn't allowed to come. They didn't want me around because I was rebellious in their eyes. My mom paid the rent for two months and arranged for me to live with a friend until I found my own place. Again, she chose her husband over me and it just made me feel even more insecure. My older brother was there but he wasn't. Here I was just 18 years old with a scholarship to go to college. I was supposed to be feeling amazing - *on top of the world*. But instead, I felt so unsure of myself and the world around me. I felt so all alone.

    Shortly after being on my own, I started working. The financial responsibilities were now on my shoulders.

    I bounced around a lot from one house to another. I never stayed in one place for too long because the people who I lived with would kick me out or steal my rent money. I couldn't rest my head for too long anywhere because nowhere was ever safe. I was working and going to school full time.

    They say an idle mind makes for the devil's playground. Well, he was playing, and I enjoyed it. I had no direction and I felt that I needed excitement. Men became my focal point. It felt good being wanted and needed. Even if it was temporary it was better than nothing. I knew *nothing* all too well. I didn't want to go back to that.

While working I met a guy who wanted me to date his brother. Without a thorough background check, I obliged. His brother quickly became my boyfriend and I started doing everything. Drugs, sex, you name *it*; I indulged. I was filling voids. My mother abandoned me, my father was dead, and my oldest brother was in the streets. I had nobody.

5

Rape

This part of my story isn't easy to talk about but with the Lord, there isn't any trauma too hard for Him to heal.

Shortly after living on my own, I was involved in a relationship. It was fun. It was everything I needed at the time to validate my existence... so, I thought.

The guy who I was dating picked me up from work one day and told me he had a surprise for me. He said he wanted to take me out for dinner and treat me because I was such a great girlfriend.

Mind you, I had just gotten off work and I thought we were going out to dinner, so I mentioned that I needed a change of clothes. He told me not to worry because he would take care of it.

In my mind, I thought he had a surprise back at his place. We headed back to his apartment and I was eager to get upstairs. We went upstairs and I took a shower. I still didn't have a change of clothes. When I got out of the shower, I noticed that his brother and friend were there. I had no idea they were coming. He had not informed me.

A sinking feeling quickly hit my stomach because I realized then that I was being set up. I was beaten and raped by all three of them. Whatever little innocence I had left was stripped from that assault. After the attack I was kicked out from his apartment. This was the same guy who I thought I could trust. *He was my boyfriend and he just kicked me out after raping me.* Not only did he do it, but he allowed his brother and friend to do it also.

I was so traumatized from this. I didn't have anybody to talk to about what just happened to me. I didn't know who else to call so I called my brother and he picked me up. When he picked me up, he had a gun laying on his lap and a couple of his friends with him. He asked me what I was doing on this side of town and I quickly made up a lie about my friend's car breaking down.

That car ride was the longest ride of my life. My older brother was the epitome of *bad*. I could have easily told him what just happened to me and he would have taken care of them. He didn't mind shooting anybody. He walked around with guns all day and the company he kept did so as well.

Revenge was literally sitting right next to me, but I couldn't do it. As much pain as I was in, I didn't want to see my brother get in any trouble, much less kill anybody. So, I fought back tears and never told anybody what happened to me that day.

How do you overcome such a trauma? These three scriptures came to mind and helped me to overcome:

> "You shall not take vengeance, nor bear any grudge against the children of your people, but you shall love your neighbor as yourself: I am the Lord.
>
> Leviticus 19:18

Now, I didn't like this verse. I was just the victim of rape. So, are you telling me, I *still* have to love?

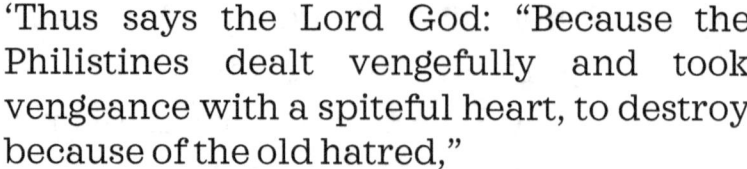

> 'Thus says the Lord God: "Because the Philistines dealt vengefully and took vengeance with a spiteful heart, to destroy because of the old hatred,"
>
> Ezekiel 25: 15

This scripture gave me a better understanding of what God was saying to me. The Philistines' heart posture was always coming from a place of vengeance. Vengeance indicates you have a spiteful heart. I couldn't deny that. But the next scripture He revealed to me, gave me the reassurance I needed.

> Dearly beloved, avenge not yourselves, but rather give place unto wrath: for it is written, Vengeance is mine; I will repay, saith the Lord.
>
> Romans 12:19, KJV

Two months after the sexual assault, I was informed by the guy who introduced me to my assailant that there had been an emergency. Upon arriving at the hospital, I was told the three men who sexually assaulted me where all involved in a terrible car accident.

My boyfriend, at the time of the attack, lost one of his arms. His brother lost one of his legs and the friend was killed instantly. I cried and felt bad for them, but that day really solidified Romans 12:19. I never looked back.

6

Taking Care of My Mother

While in college I received a phone call from my stepfather that would change the direction of my life for years.

My stepdad called me to inform me that while I was away attending college, my mother had become really sick. She had gangrene in her right leg and the doctors would need to amputate some of her toes. My stepdad needed help taking care of her and asked if I would be the one to help. Even though I was hurt by my mother and the pain she had caused me, I still loved her. So, I decided to drop out of college and help take care of her. That decision was hard for me. I loved going to school. The importance of education was something my father instilled in me before he passed away.

However, the rape and the chaotic lifestyle I was living - constantly moving around and people stealing from me, had took a heavy toll on me. I was tired and needed a break. Giving up my education was not something I wanted to do but I was happy to be leaving the city and all the horrible memories that came with it.

Before I left, I met someone new. He was completely different from the men I had been used to dating. He took care of me in ways I never knew existed. It felt good to be loved. I told him what was going on with my mother and he immediately was on board to leave with me.

I started taking care of my mother full time after she had her surgery. My stepdad had not yet kicked his *habits*. He still would be gone for weeks at a time, leaving me to take care of my mother plus my two younger siblings who at the time were in middle school.

I was doing everything my mother couldn't do and everything my stepdad wouldn't do. He would not do it because finding his next high was still his number one priority. I was taking my brother and sister to and from school, plus helping my mom pay bills, and taking her to her doctors' appointments.

It was nice being needed by my mother. It was far different from the relationship we had before. Was this the love I was missing from my mother all along? Maybe her getting sick was a blessing in disguise. This is what we needed I reasoned to myself. That's what I believed.

7

Becoming a Mother

Shortly after moving back in to help take care of my mother I found out I was pregnant. I was happy at first because I was finally in a relationship that I thought was great. This was my first child, and I was having this baby with someone that showed me the love I was looking for. Unfortunately, things quickly changed and the man I thought I knew changed into someone unrecognizable. Over time infidelity and deceit became a major problem in our relationship. Even though I left him many times during the course of our relationship because of his infidelity, I always took him back. Again, the rejection from my childhood was resurfacing in my relationship with my child's father. I was so young, and I was a baby myself having a baby.

With all that I had been through, I just wanted my family to work. I wanted my baby to have stability and love. I didn't want my child to grow up in the brokenness I experienced.

The infidelity was a problem, but I took him back because he showed me he didn't mind being a provider for his family. He was a great provider but also a great cheater. Our relationship didn't get any better and escalated to manipulation. He became very controlling and started interfering with my friendships. He didn't want me hanging out with anybody and tried to cut me off from my mom.

It became really bad, and I couldn't take it anymore. So, I left him for good and moved back in with my mom. I took our daughter with me. I remember one incident in particular after I left him that turned into a physical assault. He wasn't too happy I left the relationship, but I knew I needed to for the safety of our daughter.

Unbeknownst to me, he was plotting to attack me. One night I went to the store to grab some things for a party at my daughter's school. I didn't know I was being followed by him until it was too late. When I parked at the store, he pulled up from behind me, jumped out of his car, and pulled me out of my car by the arm. He then smashed my face into the driver side door. He ended up busting my lip open and I lost my tooth. I filed an assault and battery charge against him and there was a warrant out for his arrest. He was eventually found and arrested. As a result, he lost full rights and custody of our daughter. I have been the primary parent since that day.

8

Health Issues

After the physical assault from my daughter's father, I didn't want any part of a relationship with a man. All the experiences I've had thus far with men ended in betrayal and heartbreak. They sure weren't making me feel like Psalm 139:14 which states, "I will praise You, for I am fearfully *and* wonderfully made; Marvelous are Your works, And *that* my soul knows very well." These relationships were not the reflection of how God saw me.

I focused my attention on my daughter, continued to help take care of my mom, and enrolled back into school.

Nevertheless, disaster and a series of health issues started to plague my life. One morning while making breakfast, my mom had a seizure at the kitchen table. I rushed her to the hospital, and we were informed that her blood pressure was extremely high. Shortly after, in 2016, my mom had a massive stroke that left her handicapped. I never thought that my own mother would be disabled.

This was a woman who, prior to her health declining, was totally independent, despite the amputation. She had a full-time job and was able to get around without any assistance. We used to go to church together and have spa and movie dates. We really were a team and rebuilding the bond that was broken.

After her stroke, she went to rehab for three months. She had to learn how to walk, drive, and talk all over again. She never was fully the same and walked with a limp. The stroke affected her right side and she always dragged her right foot and swung her right arm.

Over the next year, she had several more strokes and thirteen seizures. I was constantly trying to find a job that would work around her needs, her doctors' appointments, and my own daughter's schedule. It became so overwhelming for me. I was one person handling ten different jobs and getting little to no help from the people who should have been there for us.

I was still very young and had responsibilities above my capacity. It didn't matter how hard I worked; it wasn't good enough because the demands on me were so high.

My mom was a woman of faith and I saw her exercise her faith in the Lord so much during that time. I would hear her praying for hours at a time, but her health continued to deteriorate. She was then diagnosed with level five kidney failure and was put on dialysis. Also, she ended up getting a pacemaker because her heart rate kept dropping and had three more amputations. My mom was dying slowly, and I knew it.

During that time, I gained an extreme amount of weight, causing my own health to start declining. I weighed over 490 pounds. I used food as my comfort. Some of the weight was from my pregnancy and the health issues I developed while I was pregnant. I was diagnosed with severe preeclampsia, congestive heart failure, and an enlarged heart. My body was under so much pressure at only 20 years old. I really was concerned for my well-being.

My primary care provider introduced me to the term 'gastric sleeve'. This procedure removes eighty percent of the stomach. As a result, less food is able to be consumed. I needed to do something. I saw my mom's health issues and I did not want that to be my life. Also, I was tired of being overweight, so I decided to go through with it.

It would be seven months until I could get the procedure. I was meeting with a psychologist and nutritionist regularly and was able to lose 33 pounds on my own.

Once I was given the clearance by my doctors, I went through with the surgery in 2017. I was in the hospital for three days after the surgery and it took me two months to recover. Within those two months, I lost 75 pounds because I wasn't able to eat anything solid. My stomach still needed time to heal and couldn't handle solid foods. Over time, I lost 298 pounds and am glad to say, my health problems decreased substantially, and I never gained the weight back.

9

Saying Goodbye

After my surgery I was feeling good. The weight I was losing was definitely a confidence booster. So much so, that I met someone new. We were not in a relationship for long before we got married. My marriage produced my first son, and we were happy for a short time.

Throughout my life, I always felt like I could never obtain the happiness and joy I would see other people with. My life always consisted of a repetitive cycle of heartbreak, despair, and loss. When I did experience any type of joy it was short lived.

My husband at the time was a good man and was excited about being a father. He was in college and we were a young family. During that time, I was still taking care of my mother and it caused a lot of issues between him and I.

Taking care of my mother was not the issue. It was the amount of time it took up in my life. I didn't have any time to give my husband or my new marriage. Eventually, he left when I was five months pregnant with our son.

He tried to take me to court and claim that our son was not his but that proved to be a lie. He also tried to get full custody of our son, but the court overturned his request. Our marriage eventually ended after two years.

While going through these legal troubles with my ex-husband, my mother became very ill. I had to take her to the hospital. My mom had gone through so many surgeries and was always in and out of the hospital, so when the doctors said she needed another surgery, I didn't think anything of it. Surgery with her, had become a part of our everyday life. That surgery, however, was the last one she would have.

She did not recover and was brain dead. She was also suffering seizures that the doctors could no longer control, no matter how much drugs they gave her. My mother's body was completely shutting down and there was nothing anyone could do about it.

I gave birth to my second child in the same hospital that my mom, two floors down, was fighting for her life in. Two months after giving birth, I had to make the painful decision to take her off life support. My mom never got the chance to hold or see her grandson.

Being the power of attorney for my mom was bittersweet. I was the only one she trusted to make decisions for her wellbeing. The decisions I had to make, cost me everything. During her last days, we really reconciled from the past hurt and pain I endured at her hand, all the while, I was going through a divorce and just gave birth to my son. All in one breath. I could not breath.

On March 5, 2019, I took my mom off life support. I was surrounded by my friends and family. I received donations from so many people to help cover the cost of her funeral, which helped me out tremendously during such a painful time in my life.

So many people showed up for her funeral, but nobody was there when she was sick. Where were they when I was pregnant and needed help taking my mother to and from her doctor's appointments? I was so angry because these same people who showed up for her funeral, were not there when I needed help for her.

The biggest hypocrite of them all was my stepdad. I couldn't stand him the most. He was part of the problem. I wanted more than anything, to give him and everybody else a piece of my mind. But I held my peace for my mother's sake and to honor her funeral.

After the lights went off, the chairs were put away, and all the well-wishers said goodbye, reality really set in. After the funeral, I remember sitting on my mom's bed with a gun - holding it under my chin. I really felt like I lost my whole world. I didn't see the point of living anymore and killing myself felt better than living. I just wanted to stop hurting. I felt *it* my whole life and my mom's death really was my breaking point.

Just when I had made up my mind and was about to pull the trigger, I heard a knock on the door. It was my daughter. She came in the room and I heard her simply say, "Mommy, I love you." There was something about the way she said it; like *it* was God Himself. That broke me down and completely stopped me in my tracks from committing suicide.

10

Rebellion

Have you ever been in a place in your life where you were fueled by anger? Where your desire was no longer to please God, but instead your flesh? That's the mental space I was in after my mom's funeral.

I hated God and could not understand why He would take my best friend and comforter away. I was so blinded by my own selfishness, that I could not process reasonably. I was so hurt, broken, and lost that I could not see past my own trauma.

I became something... *something* I wished no one would ever know about. For about 3 years I used sex to fill every void in my life. I downloaded all the social media dating apps I could and developed an unquenchable desire for sex. I would meet men through these apps and engage in sexual relationships. The bible states in James 1:14, KJV, "But every man is tempted, when he is drawn away of his own lust, and enticed."

Nobody was forcing me to engage in these actions. I went looking. Satan presented the opportunities, and I took the bait. 1 John 2:16 states, "For all that *is* in the world—the lust of the flesh, the lust of the eyes, and the pride of life—is not of the Father but is of the world." The desires of the world became my focus. I was far from the God I *used* to love and believe in.

My wakeup call didn't come until I became pregnant with my third child. I was so humiliated, upset, afraid, and dumbfounded. I did not want the responsibilities of another child. What made it worse was when I told the man I was involved with that I was pregnant, he packed up and left me. Here I was again, a single mom of now three children.

The weight of my actions, because of the lifestyle I was living, really started to convict me. I was not only having sex but unprotected sex. I barely was using any protection or going to the doctor regularly to check my status. Now the fear of sexually transmitted diseases started to way heavy on my conscience as well. *Have I put my unborn child and myself in danger?* I cried and cried and thought about having an abortion or giving my baby up for adoption.

No matter how hard I tried to reject the idea of this child, God would not let me do it. I thank God for His mercy because even in all my ways, and years of rebellion, He covered me. I never contracted any diseases and as I started to attend my ultrasound appointments, I began to fall in love with the blessing God gave me in my dark hours.

I gave birth to a beautiful baby boy and I named him Noah. Even though my third pregnancy was not something I initially wanted, God used it for my good.

I realized I couldn't lay down with dogs and not get up with fleas. We do not get to choose what we will receive from a lifestyle of sin. But it's guaranteed, you'll receive a portion that you don't like. It will either humble you enough to repent and turn from your wicked ways or lead you to death.

I'm reminded of 2 Chronicles 7:14, "if My people who are called by My name will humble themselves, and pray and seek My face, and turn from their wicked ways, then I will hear from heaven, and will forgive their sin and heal their land." The act of true repentance and change is an action that can't be faked because your lifestyle will tell on you. The choice is yours, but God cannot and will not operate in sin. He is holy and has no jurisdiction in the place of sin. As His children, we are called to live, operate, and embody His holiness.

I had some internal changes to make, and I knew they needed to be done. So after giving birth to Noah, I really focused on healing and building my relationship back up with God. The Lord gave me three precious reasons to keep pushing forward. I didn't want to let my children or God down.

11

My Struggles

A month before my mom passed away, I became really close to my aunt. She was my father's sister. I remember being on the phone with her for two hours and it was amazing. She was the only real connection I had to fill in the gaps and answer the questions I had about my father. My father died when I was eleven years old, so I didn't really get the chance to know his side of the family. It was nice talking to her and reconnecting to a side of me that I never could get from my mother.

I had a plan to go see her and the rest of my family, but the timing was horrible. I just had my second child and was still taking care of my mom full time. I couldn't squeeze in the time because my schedule was so full.

Thankfully, we really did build a close relationship through our telephone calls. After one conversation particularly, she told me to call her the following day to give her my address because she wanted to send me some things for my baby. Unfortunately, that would never happen. I called her the following day and to my surprise someone else picked up the phone. I knew instantly something was wrong because she always picked up her phone.

I was informed that after the last time we spoke, which was the day prior, she passed away in her sleep following our phone conversation. I was shocked. I wasn't able to make it to her funeral because shortly after she passed away, my mother passed away, as well as a cousin of mine.

Death came in threes for me, and I could not focus. I was filled with so much grief. I slipped into a lifestyle of sin to try and fill the voids and pain I was carrying but *it* never satisfied me. Nothing satisfied me. It didn't matter how many men I slept with, after we were done, they left and I still was all alone. I still was unhappy. The momentary pleasures never could heal my internal wounds.

I found myself at a real low place and had lost so much weight. I even contemplated suicide. No matter how many times I tried to take my own life, the Lord intervened somehow, *someway*.

I was reconnected to a church and God's people, which really helped build me back up. They saw my brokenness. They saw my struggles of being a single parent. They saw the grief I was carrying from losing three family members back-to-back and spoke life into me.

That is all I needed. For so long I had to do everything on my own; and for so long all I needed was help. For someone to believe in me. They really encouraged me in the Word of God and helped me find resources to pay my bills. I am forever thankful for my brothers and sisters in Christ the Lord, who He sent my way to build me back up.

12

Being a Single Mom Through It All

I've lost track of how many days I had to carry groceries while being pregnant; load and unload the car by myself; and journey with my trash to the dumpster. A lot of people don't think twice about these responsibilities, but for me these were tough tasks. Especially when my kids were still very young.

    I remember working eleven hour shifts then immediately going straight into 'mommy mode'. Pulling a whole additional shift in 'mommy mode' includes, but is not limited to: doing laundry, cooking, cleaning, and making sure my kids are prepared for the next school day. This became my life. A lot of times I wouldn't get into bed or take a shower until early in the morning the following day. There were days when I wanted to throw in the towel, but I knew God would not give me anything I couldn't handle. More than anything, I knew there was nothing He would not help me with. So, my response was to keep on pushing no matter how hard it became. Some days I struggled more than I would have liked to, but I knew I had responsibilities. My innocent and defenseless children needed me to persevere. I know I have been chosen to be their mother. I love my children and want to give them the quality of life they deserve.

These truths still didn't negate the days where it was hard being the only parent, or the loneliness I felt. Those were very real emotions I would feel and could not ignore. However, I am grateful to God because regardless of my circumstances He has looked out for me thus far.

My children are a product of my choices and I can't fault God for that. But what He has done is given me the strength to take responsibility; knowing that every day with them, as their mother, is truly a gift. My mother constantly chose her husband over my siblings and me. The cost was too great because the outcome for me personally left me shattered. I didn't want that for my children so I did what she could never do, be a single parent and trust in the God that I read about and believe in. He has provided. He does provide. And He will provide. He hasn't failed me yet!

13

Having Standards

It took me a long time to understand why it is important to have standards as a woman. For a long time, I used to just date anybody and accepted any type of attention a man gave me. Of course, these relationships weren't even relationships, but sexual encounters (with the exception of my first two children's fathers). I want to express the dangers these types of relationships have, not only on your body, but mentally, emotionally, and spiritually.

A lot of my insecurities developed in my childhood and adolescence and stemmed from the poor example my mom set before me. We learn what to accept from our mothers and I don't think my mom realized the foundation she was setting for her children. Growing up, I saw my mom married to a man who had a drug addiction. He did as he pleased, was in and out of the household, and verbally abusive, yet still, my mom stayed with him.

My standards of men became exactly what I was shown by her. Nevertheless, I cannot place all the blame on her. After a certain age, we make decisions to either accept or reject the standards of love that were set before us. We can rise above the flaws in the foundation.

I realized after some time I was settling for less. I needed a major shift in my mind. First, in how I saw my body and what God intended it to be used for. Secondly, in how I looked at men.

My body was not a dump and I needed to stop allowing these men to literally deposit in me then leave. They were leaving me with their seed but didn't care enough about me to help raise their children. I was disposable to them. Sex wasn't designed to fill my voids and that's exactly what I was using it for.

I needed to stop looking at men like they were my savior. The fact that I was having sex with multiple men, who I did not know, showed how fragile my confidence and self-esteem were.

A man, especially one who is interested in you, is supposed to hold you in high regard. He will not be ashamed to bring you around his friends or family.

I realized I wasn't presenting myself as a neatly presented package. Instead, I was presenting myself as an unwrapped gift that was already presented to everybody else.

The bible tells us in Proverbs 18:22, "*He who finds a wife finds a good thing, And obtains favor from the* LORD." Men weren't finding a wife in me and I realized more than anything I needed to change.

Sex is temporary and can be very empty when you abuse the meaning it was designed for. You can be very disconnected from a person while using their body. That is what casual sex is; to appease your flesh. I caution you against doing that.

I would have sex with different men, sometimes more than three men in a week. We weren't doing anything but appeasing our flesh. It's important to remember that your rubies are precious and shouldn't be given out so easily.

Growing up, I didn't look like what the average man in society was attracted too. I was skinny, with short hair, and my skin was dark. I was not curvy, and my features made me feel even less desirable to men. That is why it's dangerous to seek attention because you become everything *but* who God intended you to be.

Society will always have certain standards of beauty. I messed up by measuring my standards of beauty to the world's blueprint and never measured them to the Word of God. The world's standards will always be superficial; however, the Word of God is eternal.

I want to encourage you to look past yourself - what you have and what you *think* you don't have. Remember, to have only a piece of the diamond is robbery. God created His daughters to have the whole diamond. You deserve the whole diamond.

14

My Last Thoughts

I know what it's like to be treated like you don't matter. I know what it's like to be the last or the afterthought... after everybody else has been picked. I know all too well the feeling of isolation and not feeling important or loved by anybody.

The love of Christ keeps pushing me forward and reminds me that I am important, *that I do matter,* and so do you. The most important thing I've learned on my journey thus far is to always know who you are and where you stand in God.

Having confidence is important because people will always have something to say: good or bad. But you must know and believe regardless of what people say, God will always be there. The Lord told me one day that *I'm qualified*.

Sometimes when we hear that phrase, we think God is talking about us being qualified to obtain *things*, but I realized that it is way deeper than that. In spite of my trials and tribulations, I'm qualified to experience the love of God. I'm qualified, in spite of what happened to me, what I did, and what the enemy tried to do with my life. I'm qualified for the promises of God and nobody has the power to take that away from me or you.

I am learning to trust God and I really encourage you to do the same. His timing is perfect. His will for your life is perfect. In Him, you will not and cannot fail in life. In Him, and nobody else, will you have full fulfillment in life.

The God of the Impossible

I am thankful for the help God has sent me during my journey. In 2019 my story was featured in a publication by an organization called Community of Hope:

A Home for Christmas

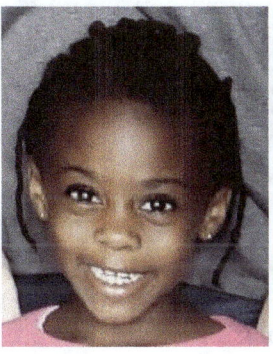

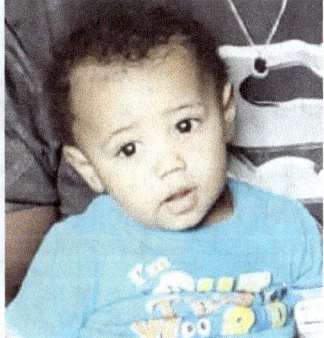

Shortly before Thanksgiving, Raven, a hard-working mother of two little ones, Destiny age 5 and Kye 10 months, found herself in the middle of a divorce, had just lost her mother, her one true best friend, and no way to pay the rent. She was forced to leave the apartment she had been in for over a year and a half to move all of her belongings into a small storage shed and to live out of her car with her two young children.

Through the referral system, 2-1-1 Brevard, she was connected to the SOS (Safe Overnight Stay) program at Community of Hope and Case Manager, Nicole. Nicole worked with Raven every single day before she entered into the SOS Shelter in Melbourne a wait due to no vacancy. Once the SOS Program had an opening, Raven gladly accepted the shelter. She would have a bed for her and the kids to sleep in at night. From there, Nicole and Raven hit the ground running. Making calls to other local agencies, reaching out to private landlords and apartment complexes, they kept hitting the same (and all too common) roadblock: the rental units all required between three to four times her income to even be considered. Working

full time still was not enough to hit that requirement.

While in SOS, Raven saved every penny she had in hopes that she would have enough for a place when she found it. Nicole referred Raven to the Coordinated Housing Assessment Team (CHAT) for rental assistance and she was approved to have her first month rent and deposit paid upon finding an affordable place in her price range. With a great deal of diligence and prayer a unit meeting her needs was found and Raven was APPROVED! Lots of tears of joy and happiness would follow. With tears streaming down her face, she would repeatedly question, "Is this really happening?" Reassurance was given and the plans for the future she'd created would be set into motion.

Raven and her children have moved into their apartment and they have a place they can call "HOME"... just in time for Christmas. They will continue working with Nicole for at least the next six months to make sure that the family gets the support and guidance they need to stay housed.

Retrieved from https://www.hopeofbrevard.com/index.php/stories/ on 4/3/21.

Therefore, if anyone *is* in Christ, *he is a* new creation; old things have passed away; behold, all things have become new.
                              2 Corinthians 5:17

2021

Stay in Touch

But as for you, you meant evil against me; but God meant it for good, in order to bring it about as it is this day, to save many people alive.

Genesis 50:20

    I am eager to fulfill the call of God on my life. My goal is to use my testimony to share the gospel of Jesus Christ and help as many people as God graces me to reach.

    Please connect with me on social media or email so we can continue to encourage one another. I have availability for motivational speaking engagement and to set-up book clubs:

<u>Facebook:</u>
    Raven Caples
<u>Instagram:</u>
    Raven Caples
<u>Email:</u>
    faithoverdestiny27@gmail.com or
    Godoverrichesfaitgfully77@gmail.com
<u>YouTube:</u>
    Search: In the Shadows of God
    Direct Link:
    https://youtu.be/J9w5qV3ocFc

I am hosting a fundraiser to help young women in need. The money raised will be used to provide them with care packages of essential items, such as, hygiene products along with other personal and household items. I am also coordinating with multiple agencies to create an up-to-date local resource guide for families in need.

My desire is to distribute this book, *In the Shadows of God*, free of charge, to women who are in shelters or treatment programs; incarcerated; or who are financially unable to purchase a copy.

In addition, this funding will help with travel expenses for speaking engagements, so that I am able to impact as many young women as possible.

If you are willing and able to financially support this mission, please make a donation, as noted below or email me for more information:

<u>CashApp:</u>
$ShadowsofGod

<u>Go Fund Me:</u>
gf.me/u/zptjzf

Thank You & God Bless,

Raven Simone Caples

www.ingramcontent.com/pod-product-compliance
Lightning Source LLC
Chambersburg PA
CBHW071407070526
44578CB00002B/509